Photographs

Linda McCartney

mpl

First paperback edition
published in the United States by MPL Communications Ltd
Distributed by Simon & Schuster
A division of Gulf and Western Corporation
Simon & Schuster Building
Rockefeller Center
1230 Avenue of Americas
New York, New York 10020

Typography and book production by Roger Huggett
Manufactured in The Netherlands

ISBN 0·671·45986·4

I am especially grateful for the contribution
made by Brian Clarke and Robert Fraser
in the preparation of this book.

LINDA McCARTNEY

PHOTOGRAPHY had to come into my life. Reading books is something I find hard to do–I'd rather be looking at, and taking in life's visual pleasures. That is why you will find few words in this book.

I grew up in a suburb of New York City and went to high school in the 50's. I had tuned my ears to Alan Freed's radio show–he played all the great Rhythm and Blues, and later the best Rock'n Roll, and I used to go to the Brooklyn Paramount to see and hear my favourite singers, musicians and groups. My father has a great appreciation of painters and paintings so at an early age I was exposed to many paintings and art books containing works of the great masters, and more modern painters. Summers were spent by the sea, and surely this helped to open my eyes to more of nature's wonders.

As a child I was animal mad, expecially about horses. I spent any free time at a local stable where pleasure for me was being with horses. Sitting on a horse's back is a great way for me to see and feel my environment–I take photos while riding, and often out of car windows.

A black sheep at home, I barely graduated from high school, but somehow managed to go to college and major in Art History. Then luckily I became a 'free spirit' in one of the most visual states in America–Arizona–exploring the foothills, witnessing sunsets supreme. While I was there I took a short photographic course given by Hazel Archer at the Tucson Art Center. The time must have been right for fate to introduce me to the camera and the appreciation of my favourite photographers: Dorothea Lange, Edward Curtis, Steichen, Steiglitz, Ansel Adams, Edward Weston, Elliot Porter, Henri Cartier-Bresson and so many more.

After Arizona I returned to New York and began taking photographs as a career. For me, the child who never seemed to do anything right, taking pictures was a natural. I found great pleasure in looking, and through a lens I could see, and therefore capture, moments–making them into memories.

I have seen paintings and photographs depicting the horrors of war, the slaughter of animals for human gain and sport, and man's general persecution of his fellow living creatures be they human or animal. I don't think the world has changed much because of these visuals, but I do hope they are making the world more aware of the suffering that exists. At the same time I feel that capturing day by day happiness and warmth is also important for a balanced outlook. I am a great believer in the expression 'every picture tells a story'.

LINDA McCARTNEY

Plates

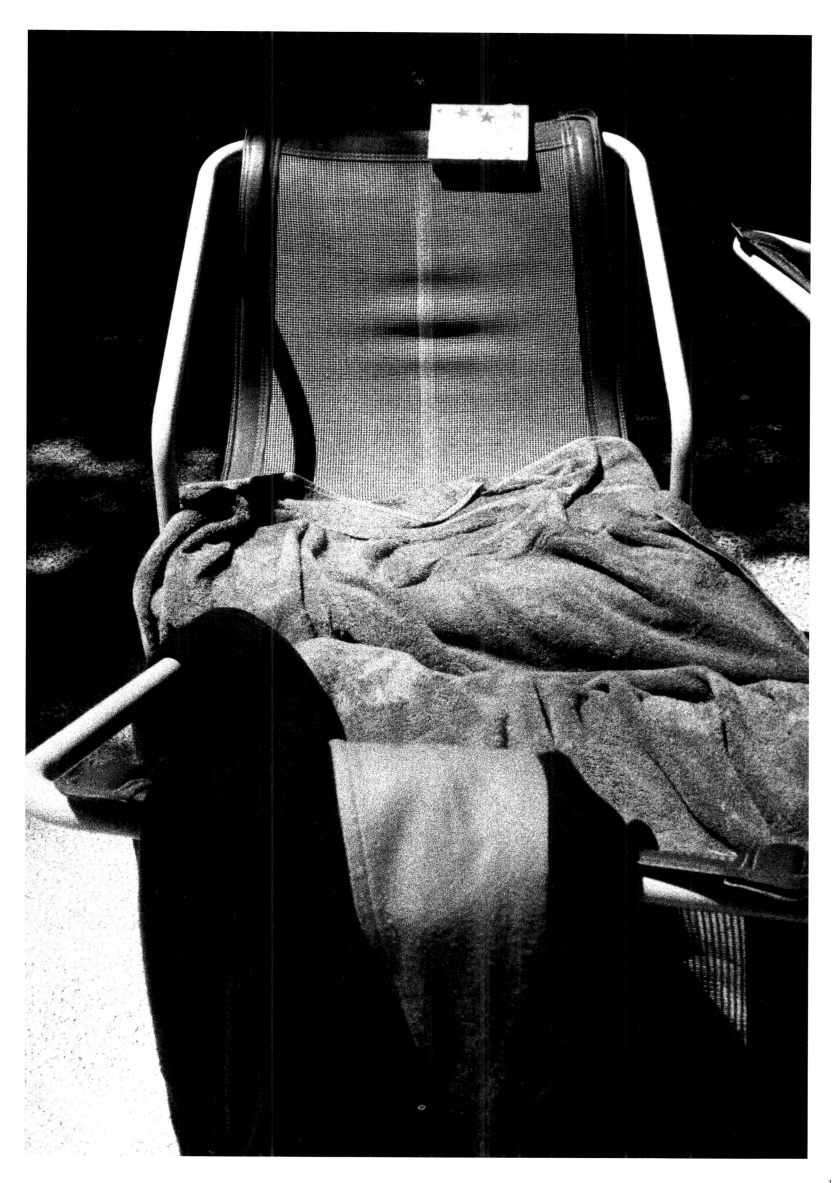

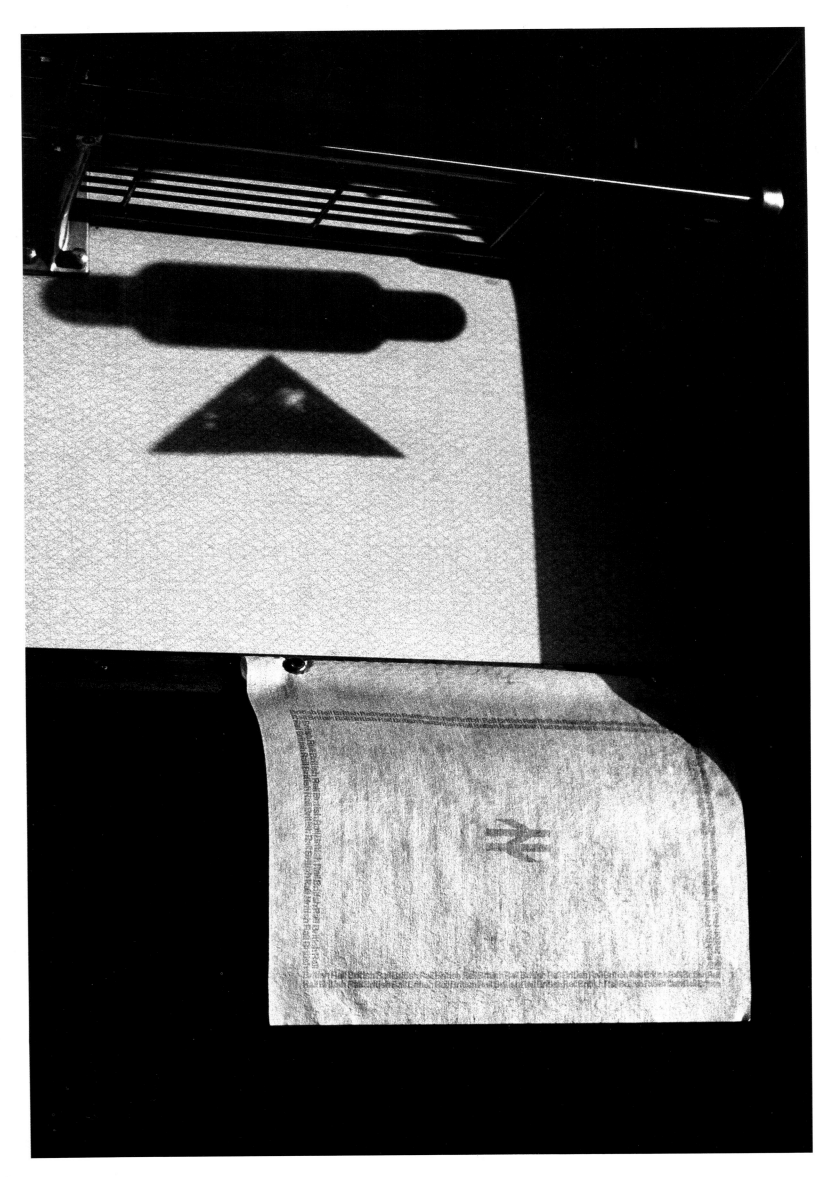

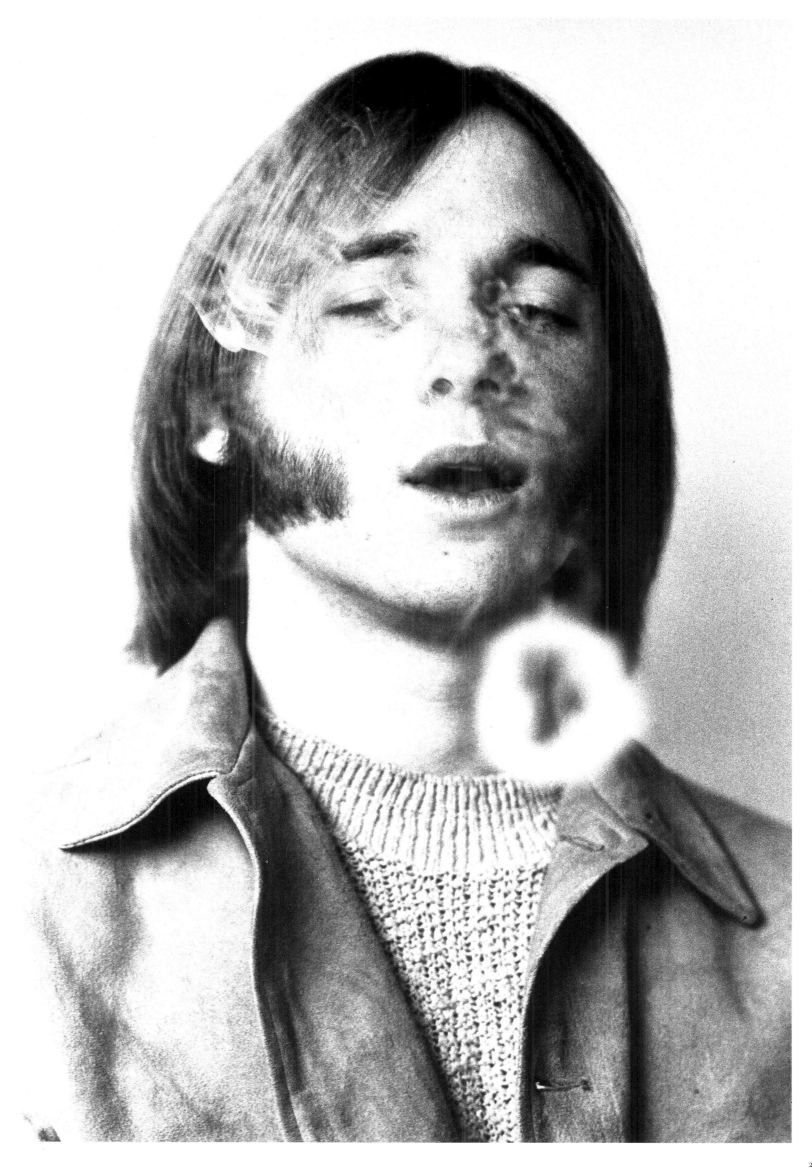

41

99

List of Plates